Empty Pages

Empty Pages

Inside the Mind of ~Z~

Zebadiah Sprague

Illustrious Illustrations
Creative Writing
Illustrious Illustrations
Photography

Illustrious Illustrations LLC

Dedicated to
A life-long journey, inspired by
Love and Compassion

Rest your heart, your soul, and your
Love in Peace Dianna!

Thank you for being the purpose
Of my path, I Love You!

~Z~

Acknowledgements

To all of the people who have encouraged and
supported me,
The ones who have inspired me and have been
inspired by me,
The ones who touted me and the ones who
doubted me,
The ones who gave me reason to investigate who
I truly am,
The ones who cultivated the best and worst parts
of me,
The ones who serenaded and persuaded the
creativity within me,
The ones who fanned the flames when they'd all
but died out,
The ones who have taken the trips with me into
my visions,
The ones who crave to see the way I see and feel
the way I feel,
The ones who have taken the time to really know
me, and
The ones who have given me the honor of truly
knowing them in return,
The ones who continue to push me, to and
through my potential

Just know that I SEE you,
I know who you are,
and I appreciate you!

After reading this book and
understanding what I can
do with words,

Hopefully who I am within
each of your lives, speaks louder
than my words ever could!

Thank You!

~Z~

CONTENTS

CONTENTS

CONTENTS

CONTENTS

NOTES

NOTES

PREFACE

Anthology (Noun):
A collection of selected literary pieces or passages or works of art
(Merriam-Webster)

People often question why I am the way that I am, or they sometimes say things like, "It's intriguing to see the way your mind works" – simply because I tend to think about things in ways or ask questions that very few people choose to consider. Some have even said that they've never met someone who thinks the way that I do or dives as deeply into things as I, so often, do. "Yeah, but you're different and we've talked about this" is the response that I often get when I share my thoughts or opinions.

The following content is a collection of pieces that I had written over a span of two years while taking a three-year sabbatical from relationships to investigate why I am, in fact, who I am. I spent the tertiary year immersed in the local spoken word and poetry reading culture by attending as many gatherings as I could find. It took me awhile to find my stage presence but when I did, I found out just how much my work resonated with others, which is eventually what ignited the idea to organize my work into a collection that I could share with a larger audience.

However, I don't want you to embark with me on this journey into my story with the expectation of a happy ending in mind because there isn't one; it doesn't have a happy ending, a tragic ending, or any other ending for that matter. The ending of this book was intentionally never written so that, as you get to the place where I stopped writing, you can pick up where I left off and begin writing from wherever you find yourself within your own lives – because my hope is that I will inquire minds to go deep into their own story and find an outlet to help them acknowledge who they truly are, the sources of any struggles that they may be experiencing in life, and a way to begin healing themselves. I, personally, wasn't looking for any sort of redemption from others as a result of my writing and I wasn't hoping for the reconciliation of any lost connections that I once had either. I needed to know and under-stand myself, from the core of who I am. I needed to learn about why I make the choices that I had made in life, why I walked down the paths that I had chosen to walk in the past, and how to teach myself that I can change those traits within who I am – so that I can essentially change the paths of my future.

Through poetry, spoken word, short story writing and random concept blogging – I found creative writing to be an incredible way for me to get my emotions and swirling thoughts out from within me and into a medium that I could share with others in a way that connects with them on a level that they understand or better yet – feel. When you are able to put your emotions into a format that allows others to see how you think and how you feel, they are then able to see 'Who' you are. More importantly, if you're able to reach them in a way that allows them to 'feel' the emotions and/or mental state of who you are then they potentially have the ability, the intrigue, and the drive to pursue the same exploration into themselves with a similar craving for understanding who they are, why they choose the paths that they have chosen in the past, and how to change the direction of the paths they will choose in order to begin rewriting the story of their own future.

The title (and essentially the entire concept) for this book came from within its first entry, a spoken word piece that I had written surround-ing the idea of helping others find a way to navigate through their emotions, through their pain, through their struggles, and essentially into themselves; not shying away from what you find but understanding it and then sharing it with the world so that they, too, can understand who you are.

How it all began for me was through my acknowledgement of the way that my mind was captivated by certain words, phrases, segments of song lyrics, ideas, concepts, random thoughts, questions, metaphors, idioms etc. My mind wanted to expand on those things because I could feel them internally, on one level or another, so I would write them down on anything I could find close by: envelopes, scratch paper, junk-mail, sticky notes and so on. That way I could eventually return to them, digging deeper into why they grabbed my attention, and then write something in a way that would allow you to see what happens inside my head or possibly even understand who I am as a person because I had found a way to give you the chance to feel what I felt. It's about reaching people on their level, or a level congruent with your own, in a way that encourages them to not only do the work within their own lives but also to invite you in so that you can understand who they are as well. It's the same way authors, poets, musicians, song writers, film producers and many other artists find ways of self-expression that grasp your attention, tell you a story, share their emotions or help you find a way of putting meaning to your own. This was the conceptual purpose of having 'Empty Pages' throughout the process of sharing my story and experience with you. These are just a few intentional spaces for you to jot down any thoughts, emotions, ideas, or inspirations that will hopefully lead to explorations of your mind and encourage you to invite others down into who you are as well; far too often, people are afraid of opening up about who they are and/or allowing others into their most vulnerable states of being.

The fact that this book has no intentional destination or ending plays a crucial role in its actual intention. As described in the first lyrical entry of the book, we tend to read books from beginning to 'End' and then put them on a shelf, give them away, or return them to the person or place from which we borrowed them. Yes, we enjoyed them; Yes, they consumed us for the time it took to 'Finish' them; Yes, sometimes they can be good enough to make you pick them up again somewhere down the line – but, so often, "books that get read from front to back" serve their purpose and then we move on. I wanted something more from this anthology of my thoughts. I wanted it to encourage its readers to return to it anytime they needed inspiration, drive, or help navigating through their own thoughts and emotions. I wanted to inquire into others about their own thoughts and feelings. My hope is that within each piece of my writing I am able to, at some point (or several points) "stop time, or at least slow it down for a moment" by inducing thoughts and provoking emotions that spark the creativity within others.

Realizing that I had encountered so much of my inspiration from bits and pieces of several different sources that had unknowingly given me a starting point from which to begin creating my work, I began using the metaphor of an unfinished puzzle that one might find in a lobby, waiting room, or library as a way of describing what I was trying to create. Someone picks it up and starts putting it together – either from a corner, from an easily identifiable section of the bigger picture, or by confining the entire concept with a completed border section – and then leaves it partially constructed so others can add to it. I, myself, have always loved the challenge and subsequent feeling of achievement derived from puzzles with one thousand pieces. I would frame them and hang them in my home once they were completed. Though I preferred brand new ones, I would also eagerly jump right into the journey of used or recently disassembled puzzles of equal size – sometimes never knowing for sure if all of the pieces were even there. That didn't matter much at the time because my passion to create and my drive to see the beauty of what IS there insisted that I pursue each challenge with a determination to reach creative completion as quickly and efficiently as possible. This analogy is exactly how I viewed every note or scribbled concept that I had collected. Each idea was the bottom left corner, or even a largely completed section, of a puzzle with one thousand pieces that someone had already started for me. Once a puzzle is started it is much harder to deny the temptation of adding to it or even completing it. Procrastination is much easier to excuse when the puzzle rests inside its box, out of sight and out of mind or at least not antagonizing the obsessive-compulsive tendencies that beg you to address its unfinished state of being. That metaphoric description is what I chose to use as an explanation for the intention of publishing this collection of my work – and its Empty Pages; so that those of you who read it will be able to use any thoughts, ideas, concepts or emotions that my work might possibly evoke from within you - as an already started section of the puzzle that you choose to create for yourself or to share with others as an invitation into who you are.

"It's my plan and desired goal to share the story of a man who bares his entire soul in an attempt to inquire minds because, somehow, I think that if it's written in ink, it could be the link that will inspire rhymes." ~Z~

INTRODUCTION

Someone recently asked me the question:
"Why are you single?"

Although at this point in my life the answer would be that it is by choice, I will say that it wasn't supposed to be that way. My journey started at age thirteen, when I lost one of the most amazing friendships I had ever known. It was the kind that kept you up late into the night, talking on the phone, until one of you fell asleep. The kind that made her feel safe while staying in a home without electricity, due the recent storm knocking out the power, as long as I was there with her. She was sixteen and she was my first true love but there was something that kept us apart – her loyalty to an abusive and unloving boyfriend. She felt that she owed the relationship some sort of devotion and dedication toward making it work simply because she had given her virginity to him.

On May 21, 1997, I came home to my father sitting me down and trying to find the words to tell me that Dianna was gone – that her boyfriend had taken her life. When the story later unfolded, I learned that it was the result of his supposed attempt to frighten her because he found out that she had "put his business out on front street" by trying to get him help with his drug and alcohol addictions.

That is where my story begins.

I didn't understand how someone could do such a thing to someone they were supposed to love. Even more, I couldn't comprehend her extreme sense of loyalty to such an unhappy relationship. This planted a seed in my brain and in my soul. I made it my personal goal in life to make sure that the women I encountered would know the meaning of happiness and understand what it's like to truly be appreciated, treated with respect and to be shown real love. It was my goal to give every female that I knew a bar to set, or set of standards, that would say "This is what I deserve, and this is what I will not accept less than!"

On this journey I learned so much about women, and about love. I listened, I paid attention and I learned about what they want in life – what makes them truly happy. Most women, over everything else, just wanted to know that you care enough about them to pay close attention to who they are and to understand them. Everywhere I went, I made an effort to compliment or comment on things that I noticed. Whether it be a new set of nails they had gotten or if they had cut, colored, or styled their hair differently. I involved myself in their lives enough to know them and because I paid attention, I knew just what to say in order to make each individual female smile. I did this because I knew that no matter what was happening in their lives, for that moment, I gave them a reason to smile. It very well could be the only time they would smile that day.

Soon my memory began to grow, and I could remember so many things about so many people, simply because I cared enough to pay attention. Whether it was surprising you with a bottle of Wild Honeysuckle perfume because you had once told me that one of your favorite childhood memories is the smell of wild honeysuckles; or remembering, after almost fifteen years, that you would only eat the purple skittles because they were your favorite; or leaving a bag of Peanut M&Ms on your doorstep in the middle of the night because you mentioned you had a craving for them earlier that day; or randomly bringing you a maroon speckled Stargazer Lily that you would get compliments on throughout the next few days as it bloomed *and then* making it a point to do it on the same day every year; or showing up to your job before you get there just so I could leave a custom made floral arrangement along with a card and a few other things on your desk because I knew that you wouldn't have much to smile about on that particular that day; or knowing how you like your coffee, or that you prefer hot cocoa instead; or listening to the things you've never seen or done and making them happen. These are some of the things I've done for a few of the women I have encountered in my life, because I hope that it makes enough of a difference in their day and in their lives to make them smile.

My first serious relationship lasted three and a half years through high school. Holly was incredibly beautiful though extremely quiet and sheltered. This gave me the chance to show her so much about life, which also had me trying to show her so much about love. I once, secretly, bought EVERYTHING she would mention or show even the slightest interest in for the two months leading up to Valentine's Day and then I presented it to her with a visionary message. The message was not about buying her love; it was about the acknowledgement that I cared enough to listen, and I paid attention EVERYTIME her eyes lit up and her smile brightened.

When I choose to love you, this feeling and desire to make you happy only multiplies. Knowing that I am the reason you wake up smiling, live each day with a new exciting anticipation for what will happen and lay your head to rest at night feeling like the luckiest and happiest woman in the world; these are the things that make me happy. It's what I live for each day. My favorite concept is what I call "buying her chairs." Anyone who has seen the movie *Phenomenon* knows what I mean. I want to know what it is that drives you, what is your passion, and then I want to push, support, and encourage you to make it happen. A counselor once told me that this type of behavior is unhealthy and that I have a "co-dependency problem" because I NEED to know that I make you happy and I put this above taking care of myself. I disagree because my vision of Love is that if I put the safety and happiness of my partner and my kids before myself, if she does the same for the kids and me, if the kids learn to put each other before themselves - then everyone is safe and happy. Everyone gets to love and care for one another. In this vision the circle completes itself. You never have to worry about your own safety or happiness.

After Holly came six years with the mother of my first two children, followed by eight months of being single and then five years with the mother of my third child. Neither of these women was capable of living the love that I tried to give. They felt like it was too good to be real and the lives that they had lived before our relationship made it impossible for them to learn to love the way that I did. They both walked out on me, and our kids, to run back to a life of drugs, alcohol, and care-free recklessness. In an attempt to keep the women that I encountered throughout my life from allowing themselves to receive a love far less than they deserve, I had coursed a path that placed me at the receiving end of that very type of relationship.

After realizing where my journey had taken me, several months of being single preceded the day I met a woman with whom I shared a seemingly powerful connection; at least for the four months we spent together. The magnetic attraction that existed between us, way before my knowledge of her struggles, was invigorating to say the least. We had each found a new level upon which to connect with someone who peaked our intimate interests; one that induced copious amounts of endorphins, dopamine, and oxytocin – though none of that was strong enough to see us through the work that it would take to break her free of the abuse she had endured for several years before me and the manipulation she still faced as a result of that relationship. She had created two beautiful children within that environment and unfortunately those precious gifts were used to keep her from her freedom, so she respectfully told me that we could no longer continue down the path we were headed as it was essentially the main driving factor behind the manipulation being used to control her life at that point. I respected her decision and where she was within herself. She was not yet ready to set herself free, but she was very close, and I felt a sense of pride in the fact that what we shared for those few months was the beginning of growth for both of us.

I now crave for the same desire from the next woman I choose to love. A desire to constantly and consistently strive to make me smile, to improve my life, to push, support and encourage my dreams; to *buy*

MY chairs. I have not yet found a love that is dedicated and devoted to such a desire. That's why I'm single and it's where I'll be until that kind of love finds me.

To all the women who have experienced and appreciated what I've tried to accomplish over the years, I want to thank you for sharing these moments with me! Whether the relationship was one of family, friendship, coworkers, colleagues, or neighbors – I hope that I have affected your lives, even if just for a moment, enough to make you smile for a lifetime. You are the validation that who I am today is who I have always wanted to be!

Thanks for reading,

~Z~

Empty Pages

If I told you that my life is an open
Book, it would be in hopes that you'd
Pick it up and take a look. Not to read
Stories of romance, seduction, fiction
Or fantasy, but instead one that gives
You the chance to see what you can
Find when you look inside the mind of ~Z~

Forget your expectations or your predetermined
Destinations because the idea of a happy ending
Will always and forever be pending, though
Not upon my intentions nor upon attempted
Redemptions from the people that I've failed
Or the ships that have long sailed

No, this is a story filled with abundant
Intentions of empty pages for random
Thoughts and tandem descensions into
Internal dimensions that so many people
Are reluctant to share, or even mention

A book that gets read from front to back
It lacks in the fact that it gets closed
And then returned to the stack
"Ahhh Yes, that was a good book!" and
Then often never given a second look
But one that leaves you in the web it
Weaves, of endless inquiries, now that's
One that can stop time, or at least slow it

Down for a moment while still in its prime
It abandons the concept of plot and scheme
Or (dot-dot-dot) now you can see what I mean

I'm like a one-thousand-piece puzzle, that the
Broken-hearted have purchased and already
Started putting together without even knowing
Whether or not they have all of the pieces
Because it is a determination that is insisted in
The minds of the passionately twisted, though
778 out of 1000 – is the gate where the state
Of procrastination ceases and imagination
Has to replace the face of what once existed

It's my plan and desired goal to share
The story of a man who bares his entire
Soul in an attempt to inquire minds because
Somehow, I think that if it's written in ink
It could be the link that will inspire rhymes

"Empty Pages"

~Z~

Speaking in an Unspoken Language

It's my goal as a lyricist
To persist upon invoking
The notion that provoking
Emotion through what I say
Can be done when my words
Are spoken in such a way, that
Even the blind can see what's
Inside of me, and the message
Is then relayed through the many
Expressions being portrayed
By each tear that traces their
Faces, allowing each and every
Word to be heard, even by the
Ones who cannot hear, because
Tears can make a profound sound
Even when they fall upon deaf ears

"Speaking in an Unspoken Language"

~Z~

The Flight of an Eagle

I was drawn to them from deep
Down inside. I saw through all
Of the pain that they tried to hide
There were bits and pieces of
Better things and I knew that
Underneath it all was Beauty
Waiting to spread her wings

Support, encouragement
Understanding, companionship
Love and lust... these were just
A few of the things I brought into
Their devastated lives, yet the
Reward for my trouble can be
Found in the rubble and dust
For none of them had what it
Takes to be faithful, devoted
Loyal and reciprocating wives

"I held you on a pedestal"
This can be said about them
All - but in exchange for being
Risen I would subsequently
Have to fall. Taken for granted
I had lost myself in the darkness
Of the night. Only when I began
To explore the sunrise, did I find
That I could no longer ignore
What I had come to realize

I had to let them all go
And learn to fly solo, so
That I can return to the
Sky, flying high, so high
That I begin soaring with
Eagles instead of sitting
Below shitting seagulls

"The Flight of an Eagle"

~Z~

The Calm Devoured by the Storm

I close my eyes with the incoming breeze
And your face is all that my heart sees

My ears collect the sounding of the
Pounding rain and my soul screams out
Your beautiful name with each memory as
The flashes drop me to one knee while the
Heavy rainfall crashes as if it hears my plea

Deeper, stronger, it suffocates me - that
Familiar strain. Fear returns along with the
Pain. Now my eyes are forced open and
Continue to burn because you're still
Gone and everything's still the same

The lightning flashes, my heart stops
Entrapped in the electric cage that it
Forms. Cowering from the thunder as
It crashes, causing my heartbeat to
Resume, my chest begins pounding
In harmony with the rage as it storms

"The Calm Devoured by the Storm"

~Z~

The Disposal of a Marriage Proposal

I look around me in dismay
At what has become of my life
To think that four years ago today
I almost made you my wife

If things had gone differently
That day, would you have tried any
Harder these past few years, to be
The woman that this man needs

If you were here right now what
Would you do and what would you
Say, or would you just watch - my tears
As they fall and my soul as it bleeds

"The Disposal of a Marriage Proposal"

~Z~

Where Was My Strength

Driving through the night with the windows down
Suddenly my eyes freeze on the silhouette of
A vision thought to be so far gone. My heart stops
I can't breathe. My soul drops, hoping she can't see

Before I know it, my foot lays heavy on the brake
Pedal. I feel so weak even though I'm completely
Surrounded by at least a half ton of heavy metal
There she is in the middle of the block, our eyes
Meet and then lock. I'm frozen in a state of shock

No, not another dose of this pain. I've barely made
It through the rain and here she comes again. She's
My hurricane. In the darkness of night, I can still see
That she's living another life. She steps into the light
As someone else. I don't even recognize my wife

My daughter stares, confused, yet happiness lies within
Her big blue eyes. For a few moments they share and
Converse. I wish I could press rewind or drop the shifter
And throw it in reverse - because I know what is in store
For us tonight. Pain and tears will come looking for a fight

I stand on my balcony, teary eyes to the sky, as I talk
To my Lord and ask Him to tell me why. "YOU gave
Me the strength to make the right decisions throughout
Most of my life. I haven't thrown it all away on drugs and
Alcohol, or hatred and crime, or even fortune and fame
Where was my strength to do the same, when

I decided to try and make this woman my wife
This, is my cry, my beg, and my
Plea, Lord, in your name - Amen

"Where Was My Strength?"

~Z~

She's My Addiction

My elevated heart rate can be seen through an
Intense monolog of body language. Temples
Pulsing to the beat. Jaws clenching in a hard
Line, locking into place and biting down like the
Jaws of a determined pit bull while well developed
Masculine pectoral muscles flex sporadically like
Involuntary spasms. Strong arms wrapping around
Her and fists tightening as I envelop her in the
Hate that she has helped to create...

... and now she feels my rage.

I lay her down and kneel in the apex
Of her thighs. She places one hand on my
Chest and the other around her unspoken
Desires as she places me inside her and tightly
Wraps her legs around my waist. She pulls me
Into her thrusting hips and her mouth springs
Open gasping for air. My hand caresses her
Face, cupping her jaw in my palm while using
My fingers to trace and silence her lips. With
A strong pelvic thrust she moans and tilts her
Head to the side. She's trying to hide it but she
Cannot, so she is forced to confide...

... and now she feels my ecstasy.

My teeth almost pierce the skin as my lips
Wrap around the taut muscle that travels
Down to her shoulder. My left hand still
Embracing her face while my right hand slides
Under her arm and glides up the back of her
Neck. My fingers massage her scalp as they
Run through her hair before closing around
A fistful and thrusting deep inside her. Once...
Twice... Three times, with meaning. I release
Her face and her hair, wrapping both of my
Arms underneath hers and gripping her
Shoulders as we repeat this cadence. She
Throws her arms passionately around my
Shoulders. Her hands pressing my face against
Her chest. With her legs she squeezes me so
Tight that I cannot escape the depths that we've
Reached inside her through the previous steps...

... and now she feels my pain.

My release is euphoric. When we reach climax, my
Body shivers. My muscles tremble from emotional
Weakness. My chest cavity expands as my exhausted
Lungs try to keep up. My eyes meet hers and they
Are glossy, filled with empathy. I kiss her deeply as
She holds my face in both of her hands and she
Begins to cry. When my lips release their grip on hers
She is breathless. I helplessly lay my face upon her
Silky smooth abdomen. My hands upon her breasts
And her hands upon mine. My heart rate drops and I
Close my eyes. Once again I am fine...

... and now she feels my peace.

"She's My Addiction"

~Z~

Morning Relapse

Through my eyes I can see your
Face in the reflection of the rain as
It hits the street of that intersection
So, I close them to avoid your deceit

The smell of the rain takes the place of
Your name and I feel safe again for there is
No longer a recollection of any connection to
You because it doesn't even smell the same

Once again, I am able to stand to my
Feet and as I look around, I am glad to
See that my morning relapse has been
Discrete and I'm back on solid ground

"Morning Relapse"

~Z~

Farewell to a Blinding Disease

(Adding onto a quote that I once read)

"I was your cure
But you were my disease
I was saving you
But you were killing me" -unknown

 ... the things I would endure as
You brought me to my knees, but
I often found myself craving you so
It wasn't easy to see. Although when
I knew for sure, I set sail to open seas
Leaving you behind, on dry land, waving
As I bid you 'adieu' and I am smiling now
At how fulfilling my new life will surely be

"Farewell to a Blinding Disease"

~Z~

To know you is to love you. To love
You is to die painful and slow. Slowly
Leaving behind an empty soul. A soul
That's been solidified by death. A death
That I chose to impose upon myself, for
Reasons of loyalty that nobody knows

Here I stand as a testament to a love
Story told. Told of a love that has now
Gone cold. As cold and lifeless as stone
Stone-faced in shame. In life, love, and
Death I stand the same, I stand alone

"Petrified Suicide"

~Z~

Liquid Fate

He lost a fight in the darkest alley of the
Night as he stumbled into a bottle of
Liquid fate. Swimming in it at full throttle
Until he could no longer see straight

Now just remnants of an honest man, once
Wise and despite the fight of being mentally or
Emotionally tested every other night, until now
He had been truly invested in being levelheaded

Though he was an educated soul with
Swagger and ambitious plans, he now
Stands with a dagger in his hands and
His throat rested on beveled edges

Where is the sober sanity of a man when
Even through the flickering flames he's still
Picturing her face covered in all of the men's
Names that fill him with shame as he watches
The picture frames burn in the fireplace

Who's to blame as the bottle crashes against
The wall and the memory of his wife flashes
Against the flaming ashes of his life? He's no
Longer able to stand tall. His knees are weak
And his stomach turns as he begins to fall

He staggers to his feet, savagely tearing out
This heart that he no longer needs. Unwilling

To accept defeat, he stares at it while it bleeds
Every beat covering both of his hands with the
Warmth of the liquid soul upon which it feeds

In the end his pain was relieved in
The very sin that it was conceived in
Liquid hate breeds liquid fate, and a
Liquid soul bleeds as payment of the
Toll when we arrive at the Golden Gate

"Liquid Fate"

~Z~

Empathetic Emotion

(Written after hearing a lyrical testament of one
woman's past as her video went viral on the internet)

My heart hurts. Familiar or so it
Would seem. My tears flow as I listen
To her soul scream. Flash backs to the first one
When I was thirteen. Sittin' on the same tracks
I can't stop thinking about my new queen

All the things she must've seen before and
All the pain she must've had to endure. To
Think that I can even take the pain away by
Simply showing her that today is new day

I'll never fully understand what these women
Go through but hopefully you can take my hand
And let me show you. There's a love and a life
Much brighter on the other side with no need to
Be a fighter and no pain to have to try and hide

I know it's hard to find your way through the
Mystic haze, so I'll be searching for your soul
Through this violent maze and when I find her
You will know so much more. Just take my hand
And let me guide you through that open door

"Empathetic Emotion"

~Z~

Mi Linda Palomita

These words are written
In rhythm to spoken word for
They are meant to be read but
More importantly heard

When I met you, something bit me
I cannot lie, you were extremely
Cute and really quite shy. As the
Days went by and the week came
To an end, I found that your name
Came up often as I spoke to a friend

I'm so glad that you came out to celebrate my
Birthday that night. By morning it was obvious
That there was an attraction we could no longer
Fight. I got to know so much more about you
Like that you prefer shades of black, white, and
Gray, but your favorite color is a very dark blue

My favorite, though, was your interpretation of
A dove. I learned that for you, she's a symbol
Of Freedom as opposed to our society's cliché
Representation of Purity and Love

As I learned more and more, my mind was
Blown by the lack of respect and extreme
Mistreatment that you had been shown
And the fact that true love and appreciation
Was something that you had never known

Those who know me well would say, and
I would agree, that this is where my vice lies
But I knew it the first time I saw that your smile
Resides within your eyes, so in my defense
These words are true which I have spoken
"I liked you long before I knew you were broken!"

I thought if I could just plant a seed
Within your soul and watch it grow
Then you would rise above the pain
That makes you bleed and takes its
Toll, so that I could replace it with
A true love and watch you glow

I, myself, am on a journey of my own. One that
Enlightens and heals, but I can't ignore my soul
When it constantly kneels before me, begging me
"Please, show her a love she's never known and a
Life she's never had but clearly deserves!"
I lift him from his knees and say, *"Yes"* as a small
Fear creates chaos amongst all of my nerves

Day after day and night after night
I begin to show you a new and beautiful
Light. One that never dims and makes sure
That your smile always shines bright

My intentions were to keep you shielded from
The darker side of the fight. "You focus on you and
Keep your new path in a direct line of sight, while
I endure the struggle of capturing your freedom
Breaking away the chains and shackles because
Where you're going, you're not going to need them"

When the smoke cleared and the haze
Had lifted, I saw that the tables had
Turned and the feelings had shifted
The stress and struggles could be
Seen all over your face, causing you
To pull back and ask for some space

I just want to see you fly free
Amongst the clouds up above
Even if it's not with me, just
Fly free My Pretty Lil Dove

"Mi Linda Palomita"

~Z~

Within the Pedals of a Playboy
Floribunda

Close your eyes and imagine the skies
Resting behind many mountainous rock
Formations that are merely black silhouettes
Amongst the vibrant depths of God's creations

Skies, sun-kissed with a warmth that is most
Closely described as the touch of someone's
Fingertips, followed by the caress of soft
Subtle lips as they navigate curvaceous
Terrain with the finesse of a ship that is
Smooth sailing but never confiding of the
Passionate lust that it was hiding, which
Coursed his veins at speeds that would
Provoke a midnight freight train's derailing

An orange that is both dominant and
Submissive. Fiercely overpowering the
Less prominent emotions that lie within
The mellow yellow of its core but often
Weak to the heat of the fire that traces
The tip, like the lipstick left behind by the
Permissive lips of burning desire that begs
To color you a Scarlett Harlot for the man
That you just cannot seem to ignore

In the morning when you awake to an erotic
Sunrise set against the hopefulness of an

Emerald sea, you can't help but feel the same
Colorful explosion of emotion as you look into
The eyes of devotion belonging to the man that
Still lingers sensually in between your thighs
Wrapping his fingers intentionally in yours, as
A communication and validation that you both
Realize this is a feeling you will never forget...

... much like the embrace of an exotic sunset

"Within the Pedals of a Playboy Floribunda"

~Z~

Tearing Down My Wall

A vast field - dried, lifeless, separated by
Train tracks that flow horizontally through
The middle. A crater-like ditch to the left
Where kids from all over the neighborhood
Play, build forts, and hide the things that
Their parents wouldn't want them to have

Up above the hillside cars pass from left to right
And right to left. Houses stand still behind the
Motion-blur of traffic. Enormous pines sway in
The breeze. Soft pillows of cotton break up the
Ocean of blue skies as emotion fills my eyes

All of those things fade and become opaque as my
Vision narrows back through the traffic to the
Desolate fields below the horizontal train tracks
Closer and closer until the striped fuzziness of
Blurred blinds come back into focus

The scape of your kitchen makes itself present
Through vibrating vision, flooded with tears and
Time no longer stands still as I have to make the
Decision to return to reality and find the strength
To say all of the things that I came here to say

"Tearing Down My Wall"

~Z~

Self-inflicted Captivity

That moment when you find yourself
Upon your knees and realize the strength
That you had inside was all just a tease

Feeling safe behind your newly
Built brick wall until that familiar
Feeling causes it to crumble and fall

"No, not again! I vowed to close
That door and move on!"

It's not that easy trying to trick your soul and
Prove that love is gone. You can run but you
Cannot hide. Wherever you go it will be, for
In you it was born and in you it will reside

"Self-inflicted Captivity"

~Z~

Mi Alma Silenciosa

"Como si estuviera aquí bajo de la lluvia, estoy de pie
Pero tengo ganas de caer de rodillas. La toca
Mi rostro con cariño como mis labios besan
Los tuyos. Estoy mirando por cielo y la lluvia
Me lava el dolor. Mis ojos están cerrados pero mis
Brazos están abiertos y no quiero abrir los ojos hasta
Que estes en mis brazos de nuevo, porque tu eres mi paz"

Estas palabras son las que mi alma quiere
decir a una linda paloma.

"Mi Alma Silenciosa"

~Z~

Freedom

The message brought down today
As I sit in this pew and pray, is about
Freedom: It is what binds me to you
And the more I think about it, Freedom
Is something that maybe I need too

You were a dove captive to heavy
Chains and an iron gate. I am a love
Captive to pains of the deepest mistrust
And darkest hate. It's something I'm starting
To see. Maybe you could not be free because
There's still a need for Freedom inside of me

Maybe you could see that I wouldn't be
Able to let you in until I break free of the
Pains that I hold deep within. Who am I, but
A broken man in need of the very same thing
That I tried to offer you, a chance to be freed

Although I'm hurting and feeling weak, I am still
Standing up and I know that it's freedom which I
Will also seek, in a new direction. Freedom, it is

What binds me to you and when I find it I have
Faith that you'll be there too, so I raise my glass
Toward a brand new path - and to your reflection
Here's to flying free, wherever that may be

"Freedom"

~Z~

The Friend Zone

I want to sit on opposite sides of the
Couch while drinking coffee, spilling
All of the thoughts that we tend to hide

I want to play with your hair as you lay on my
Chest in the comfort of darkness known as your
Light Rule while you listen to every word I say

I want to wake in the morning to your laughter as
I make you gourmet French toast, listening to the
Fast drip from the brewing of my favorite roast

I want to meet you in the shadows again
Before dawn, for coffee and donuts
But that's all been long gone

The Friend Zone quickly led to the End Zone but
I never cared about the score. I liked all that we
Shared before. It's that peaceful bliss that I miss.

"The Friend Zone"

~Z~

The Lifecycle of Regretful Tears

Sometimes they're born in our feet
And grow through the path in which we walk
Strength is built as they travel through the
Calf muscles with every mountain we climb
And again in the thigh muscles as we squat
To pick up more of the weight of the world

Sometimes, but not always, they take the
On ramp to an upward spiral through
The erogenous zones of pleasure that
Some call sinful while others say blissful

Nevertheless if they take that ride
They find themselves in a place where
Butterflies live, fluttering about this way
And that. Chasing the butterflies like
Three-year-old children running through
Fields of grass in the middle of spring

Chasing this feeling will lead them out of
Our stomach and into our bloodstream
Headed straight to our heart, where they
Learn about love and warmth, pain and solitude
And so many others while on what has come
To be known as the roller-coaster of emotion
Sometimes it takes you to the highest
Places you've ever seen, giving you that
On-top-of-the-world kind of feeling. Other
Times it can drop you so fast that those

Butterflies I spoke of can't escape the
Knots that bind them and cause you to vomit

This is a confusing time for them as they
Travel into our mind and learn to be analytical
Of the places they've been and the feelings
They've felt along the way. Trying to give them
Meaning before proceeding toward the door
To share them with the world, only to find
That their path down the cheek, along the
Nose, and across the lips only leads to a pillowcase
In the darkness of solitude where they're laid to rest

"The Life Cycle of Regretful tears"

~Z~

The Desolation of a Vacant Ribcage

It's a cold and empty cavity, with a dark
Invitation for depravity, that leaves a man
Helpless to a heavier gravity than he knows
Comfort is left holding a sign that reads
'For Hire' neglected by the man's own
Forbidding of his only desire and he will
Find no warmth or relief from a necrotic fire
For this is the path that he chose

"The Desolation of a Vacant Ribcage"

~Z~

Necrotic Revelation

I'm lost for the first time and it's easy
To secure the past when I'm absolutely
Sure, that I was right, death is longer than
Life and now I'm stuck, disillusioned to
The reality of how it truly was

Released from my confusion only after
Expiring, I lay in the coldest cavity, enveloped
By the earth, returning to the beginning to
Watch a rerun of the same movie over and over

Having my only enemy to keep me company
Whose seat had been reserved because I was
So blind. Excuses, though often kept secret
Would most likely be rationalized anyway

Misled by a notion that I'd take my righteous
Place in the sky, I'm left to be a hermit in the
Silent wilderness. Even if I attempted to say
That I gave it my all and really tried, an apology
Would be concealed by the security of silence

My vision is now as clear and refreshed as this
Morning's rain, though I can only despair in the
Revelation that I lay in the damp ashes of what
Little remains, as I regretfully acknowledge that

It's far too late for any chance of redemption

"Necrotic Revelation"

~Z~

If you inquire to know me, you will most likely
Find me in ink. It's where I am free to be who
I see in me. Who I once was is not so, currently

Below suffocating sands I have begun to
Sink. Now it may not show quite so visibly
But I am actually free falling, back into me

One day the outside will fade
Away and hidden inside you'll see
Truth in what I've been trying to say

"Ink Blots"

~Z~

Divine Baptism

I urge you to open the floodgates of Heaven
To wash away the pain. Like the serpent
Who sheds his skin and arises anew from
Within, asking to be forgiven for all of his sin

Open the floodgates of Heaven
... and let it rain

There is love in the rain and
There is peace in the same
Below you, at your feet, is a drain
So say goodbye to the shame

Open the floodgates of Heaven
... and let it rain

As the rain pours, from your soul
His name soars. Higher and higher
Unlocking the doors and opening the
Flood gates of Heaven to let it rain

"Divine Baptism"

~Z~

Estranged

I found myself living life as somewhat of a pessimist
Thinking I'd be more protected, because the trust and faith
In those I was messin' with had left me torn and neglected
So I locked it all in heavy cages, the lies, the deceit, the hurt
And the pain. Though captive I still remain as the war inside
Still wages, and bleeding wounds leave my vision stained

I gave up on a journey that He had given in His name
Due to the rages that resided within. Pointing the finger
Of blame at those on theatre stages, I was filled with
Disappointments of failures that fell to a greater sin. Now
As I thumb through the pages, I feel the shame as I recall
And remember the meaning of my name

Zebadiah, a gift of God, a gift of our Lord. It's a title and
A purpose that cannot be ignored. This revelation is not
From the mouth of the righteous, filled with conceit. It's
A proclamation of salvation as I stand to my feet, staring
Into the eyes of defeat and reciting the words of Luke 4:18

Admitting that I have not accomplished all of these things but
Testifying that my track record is seemingly pristine and the
Fruits of my labor have, by many, been seen. Not only seen but
Tasted and I realize now that my time and efforts have not been
Wasted. I drop to my knees and begin to cry before raising my
Hands and looking to the sky. Seeking forgiveness with these
Flooded eyes, for losing faith in my purpose, affecting the
Deepest and darkest of lives. Vowing to be strong and return
To your service as I call on the words of Psalms 147: 3 and 5

Holding onto this pain, disappointment, and guilt will
Only cause my heart to whither and wilt. So I take a deep
Breath and I decide to no longer let it reside inside. I can
Never be anything more if I keep it all buried deep in my
Core so I grab the cage doors, frantically wiggling and/or
Jiggling the key, opening the gates and setting it free

Let the gates of my heart be open and free to love again
Let the gates of my soul be filled with what once had been
Let the gates of my mind be free of betrayal, set them on a
Ship at sea and then send strong winds into its sail

I let go of it all, no longer will it weigh me down. I will awake
A stronger man I believe as I lay me down. My path once again
In plain sight, having won the battle and conquered the fight. I
Thank the Lord for my place at His side asking Him once again to
Be my guide. For my vision is restored and the strength of my faith
Is tried-and-true. All of this I confide and I confide it - in all of you

"Estranged"

~Z~

Sittin' on the Dock as I Pray

Today as I sat amongst a large congregation
Trying to receive a message sent from above
To my left read the word "Reconciliation" and in
My mind flashed the face of my BabyDove
I can't name the reason for this weekend's
Tribulation but it reminded me of a void in
My heart, a deep and dark hole
And then I saw to my right the word
"Restoration" which may possibly be
The prescription for my soul

For many years I had this purpose, this function
It seemed to leave me fully content and satisfied
I was like a winding freeway junction that was
Trying to provide a new direction of life that
Something or someone was trying to hide

Whether the addiction was drugs or alcohol
Induced, or the violent affliction of captivity
Through manipulation and abuse, I needed
Women to know they deserved so much more
And if they'd let me, I'd open a whole new door
Never concerned with making them stay, I only
Wanted to shed a little light and show them the
Way, but I'm no longer satisfied with the game
Of catch and release, you see, she held the
Light that lit the flame and gave me peace

As I looked around at these couples
Worshipping hand in hand, I notice that
Only my children sit next to me as I stand
The symbolism is profound, he is her safe
And she is his sound. Suddenly, I look at my
Hands where hers can no longer be found, I
Begin to realize that my hands are not empty
But open, as are my eyes and I now recognize
That this is a place for Faith and not for Hopin'

Although my heart suffers from the pain of
Acidic emotion that threatens corrosion, I lift
My hands higher, out of reach from the
Oceans threat of erosion and into the
Realm of Heavenly devotion

This is definitely not about the helpless cry of
An overly sensitive and emotional guy, looking
For some kind of affirmation or consoling reply
This is just me swallowing my pride, needing the
Release of what I'm holding inside, and letting
Go of it all as I watch it roll out with the tide

"Sittin' on the Dock as I Pray"

~Z~

Mystic Mist

Ahh yes, the fog has descended
Amongst the white caps that caress
The path through the valley of pine
Simultaneously the haze is lifted
From the battlefield where a volley has
Taken place inside this head of mine

In and amongst the chaotic fight
With its sonic booms and flashes of light
I find it ironic that by driving out of the
Night and into the desolate mist
I have somehow found the place
Where peace and vision exist

"Mystic Mist"

~Z~

Dealing with a Generational Timelapse

The neglected sharpened pencil, the gentle glide
Of the ballpoint pen spilling ink across pages of a
College ruled spiral notebook. The plain black JanSport
Backpack with the brown suede leather
Bottom, a book opened and laying on its pages, leaving
The paperback cover and its binding bent like a small
Wave cap in a vast ocean. The words on the cover
Boldly say The Practice of Poetry

Above the notebook, a wide plastic rectangle with black
Plastic keys bearing white letters, a cord attached
Leads to a larger upright rectangle that streams a viral
Visual of useful resources that are offered to students
A bulbous device resembling a rodent with its winding
Tail sits adjacent to the smaller rectangle with black
Keys and white letters

A handheld piece of technology rests on the table
With yet another cord plugged into it leading to a
Large pair of headphones, the melody of smooth
Jazz streams into the eardrums of a balding man who
Sits at a cubicle with his pen and paper, his unused
Sharpened pencil, his black '90s generation JanSport
Backpack with brown suede leather bottom, his
Paperback book sprawled on its pages, his walk-man
With its cassette tape spinning inside transmitting
Brown silky tape into smooth jazz

The swarm of a much younger generation across
From him, next to him, sitting, standing, rushing
Passed him, the endless variety of devices flowing
Through their fingertips are cordless, colorful, and
Of various shapes and sizes, typing, texting, and
Drawing, no pens or pencils, no pads or notebooks
No bulky headphones or reeling cassette tapes
Just Time and it seems to be Passes Effortlessly...

"Dealing with a Generational Time Lapse"

~Z~

Staring into the Oceans at Z

Captivated by your own reflection from years passed in
The sunlight's stone deflection through the violent rain
It's an apparition that is a younger you than this time
Around, still you feel the same because you have barely
Begun your mission and are already losing ground
So, you fill the vast space of emptiness inside with shame
Asking yourself, *Is it better to fail twice or resign this time?*
Looking for some advice or some kind of sign. In
A shy cry of desperation you reach for inspiration

If you never try then you'll never know
It's better to try and fail than to never have tried at all
At least you can say that you tried
Quitting while you're ahead is not the same as quitting

But really who are you kidding, you're not ahead
At all, but instead pretty far behind. You simply
Have the presence of mind to know that you
Should humble your pride enough to choke
Down reality, because it's just too much to hide

And you nearly suffocate on the idea that
You're just not ready to take on the world
And conquer every summit or storming
Sea that stands between you and all that
You have envisioned your destiny to be

Acknowledging that right now may not be
The time to dive into an ocean of change

When she is in her prime and the future
For which you strive, is clearly out of range

Sickly infections reside inside a rapid current
That travels in several different directions
Insuring the depths of your destruction
Which lies within its succulent seduction

Is resignation then validated or are you
Just taking the easy way out? Is there any
Value in being dedicated to pushing against
The waves that crash about, repeatedly at
Your knees, warning of the dangerous road
She paves, that Vicious Vixen of the Seas

"Staring into the Oceans at Z"

~Z~

No Sleep 'til Broken

A new version of a Beastie Boys song
Keeps playing in my head. Sleep filed
For divorce, haven't seen her for a while
My mistress, Coffee, has become disloyal
Loyalty is found only in my enemy, Time
Who never lets me down. I can always count
On Time to do what Time does which is run out

I've come to realize that I cannot chase Sleep
And beg her to stay so I've moved on, hoping
To find companionship in a friend named Couch
Though she never seems to leave home, and I'm
Always too busy to visit her. The road I'm on is
Constantly busy. Traffic never slows down. The
Street sign says "Broken Blvd" with the only other
Alternative route saying "Solitude City - Next Exit"
... but the road to success has no shortcuts

"No Sleep 'til Broken"

~Z~

A Jack of All Trades

It was at The Bartlett, while in the audience of Anthology
That I became the victim of my own ideology
Suddenly I felt a sharp burning sensation
As I was slapped in the face with a new revelation
The words **But a King of None** swirled in my head
For a moment against bright sparkling flashes of light
Shaking my head and squinting my eyes, I tried to find
My opponent who was not to my left or to my right

… Standing up straight now, and much more assertive
My face still feeling pretty hot… *What the hell was that?*
I asked myself, trying to find clarity of the mind

(*Wuhluhluhluhluhluhluh*)

That's the sound I've used since way back to navigate and
Unwind the freeways of thought, like interrupting the Playback
Of a cassette tape by pressing the button that says rewind

A Jack-of-All-Trades… most people are familiar with
The phrase, which usually carries with it a positive
Connotation, though not everyone knows about the
Words that follow, *But a King of None*. They rein down
Through a thick and foggy haze, giving a once high
Self-esteem total renovation

I recall a conversation I once had with my father
Is it better to know very little about a lot, or a lot about
Very little? I used to think I knew the answer but lately
I'm finding myself somewhere in the middle
A seemingly relevant tune about a boy and his father
Proceeds to fill the room. The soulful sound of The Rustics
Tonight's feature band, brings me back to the conflict at hand

Watching musicians, writers, and poets standing before
A crowd, having already made it to the finish line. So
Many talented linguists, so many strong expressions
Of oneself, but not a single one of them is mine
I've chased so many goals and feel like I haven't
Achieved a single one. Without conscious intent
I feel like I may have become But a King of None

Waiting to be called from his corner
A rising champion sits quietly on the brink
A poet scribbles on. Emotion spilling from his soul
Only to find that his pen has long been out of ink
A passion for photography discovered and a degree
Pursued. Impressive images adorn most of the halls
Capturing his visions of life and exposing his soul as
If it were nude, yet no certificate hangs upon the wall

My first priority was a strong and stable family to soak
Up my love and pride but with a third prospective wife
Now gone, just three incomplete children stand at my side
So I set out to ride amongst the waves, caressing as much
Of the ocean as I could. I often smile knowing that so many
Women have known the true love of an honest man that's good
I just as often look at my life and wonder - What have I done?
I've become a Jack to Many Maids - But a King to None

I used to think knowing very little about a lot
Was the key because it renders you useful to
So many in need, but now I don't know. For all
My efforts, what do I have to show? So when my
Boy comes to me, with the same inquiry, what do
I say to my son when all that I have done is become
A Jack-of-All-Trades but a King of None

"A Jack of All Trades"

~Z~

Be it poetry, spoken word, or lyrical verse
Find something you can bring to the world
That breaks you free from this spherical curse

The cycle will eventually spiral down, leaving
You frantically looking around, helpless as you
Choke on your vanity and slowly drown

You were put here for a reason. Find your soul
And reach deep down to your core. If darkness
Guides you then change the season and begin
Taking back the control by opening a new door

"Soul Searching"

~Z~

Lost In You, Found In Me

For a very long time I was lost
Lost in the way your hand felt
Wrapped in mine, in the way
Our eyes met and our souls
Combined. Lost in the sensual
Moments that we'd share and
The peace you found whenever
I'd brush your hair, after intense
Sexual body massages against
Candlelit shower stalls, watching
As silhouette collages danced upon
Steaming shower walls. I was lost in
A blissful place that cannot be seen
Where intellectual conversations that
Consist of dreams and futures took up
The space that exists between all of
The motion in the ocean and the
Raging sea that persists in the lips
Hips and fingertips of you and me

I was lost in the way that we used to
Watch Everwood on Monday nights
Or go for long drives just to enjoy all of
The new scenes and sights. I was lost in
The best view in town whenever you'd
Start stirring country gravy in that tight
Black evening gown, and the extra little
Thing you'd do whenever you'd catch
Me watching you, which often led to

Things that were really quite naughty
And to many delicious adventures of
Your body. I was lost in the way that
Your eyes were the place where your
Smiles reside, or how our souls would
So often collide in the most beautiful
Place, each and every time that I saw your
Face or deeply caressed your lips with mine
I was lost in all of the things that you would
Do and say, and how everything that I did
Took your breath away. In the way that I
Missed you and how I felt when we were
Apart, or in the way it turned you on that
I'd grab your ass when I kissed you. I think
It's safe to say that we both loved that part

I was lost in you every time that you cried
And every time that you lied, until I learned
It was you who was truly lost inside and that's
When it became so clear, so evident. I began
Hearing something so Heaven-sent. The lyrics
To a very familiar song: I once was lost, but now
I'm found. All this time I had it all wrong. It was
Really the other way around. Every feeling of
Emotion and every reeling devotion, was just a
Reflection, of my own love and affection. The
Strength and power of my love always stayed
The same. The only thing that ever changed
Was your name, though your names are not
Important. We'll just call you The Past: numbers
One, Two, and Three but my eyes are now open
And it's so easy to see that I was in love with the

Way that I loved you, not the way that you loved
Me, so now that I am free of this disease, I'll pick
Up the pieces of who I used to be and pour my
Love onto the next one that makes my heart stop
And my lungs seize, because you see, although
I was lost in you... I was found in me.

"Lost In You, Found In Me"

~Z~

The Bad Influence

I want to be the one who buys your chairs
The one who supports you as you strive to
Reach your goals. The one who tells you that
You're strong and smart and encourages you
To make responsible choices. The one you can
Count on to hold your hand and walk with you
Down the right path no matter how many miles

But sometimes...

Sometimes, I want to be the bad influence that
Kidnaps you from reality, opens your mind, and
Frees your spirit. The one you can count on to take
Your hand and lead you through a few adventures
That will keep you young and create memories that
Will forever fill your life with smiles

I want to be the one to wrap my fingers in yours on
Long drives, gently caressing your thumb with mine
And sensually kissing the back of your hand. I want to
Be the one who makes you breakfast in bed and treats
You to candlelit dinners by the fire. The one who knows
Every inch of your personality and every hidden treasure
In your mind. The one who will love and respect you for
A lifetime. The one you can count on to be waiting for
You at the end of the aisle

But sometimes...

Sometimes, I want to be the bad influence that
Kidnaps you from innocence, explores your body
And seduces your soul. The one you can count on
To take your hand and lead you through the open
Door giving me the chance to explore for a while

I want to be the one who lies in between your legs
With malicious intent, kissing the skin on the inside
Of your thighs while your soul begs with delicious
Consent for me to go to the place where I can taste
The juices that flow as you fight back the urge to let
Go and let it show. Your head tilts back and your
Eyelids flutter. I can't hear the words that you begin
To mutter but it sounds something like "Ohhh Mr.
Lover-Lover" and with satin lips I begin to discover
What you try and disguise with thrusting hips and
Quivering thighs. Your hands frantically gripping the
Sheets as you try to gain some sort of control, but
You can't because my mouth practically has you dripping
And the heat of ecstasy begins to take its toll. My tongue
Creates a burning desire inside and ignites a passionate
Fire that you just can't hide. You start singing a chorus of
Deafening sounds from your climactic explosion and now
Your craving intensifies. Your body is shaking and your
Heartbeat pounds with euphoric emotion and I can
See it bathing within your eyes. Our souls meet face to
Face in this wild and erotically emotional place. The
Feelings between us are intense as I drown just the tip
In the river of your palpitation. Your stomach muscles
Tense and you bite down on your bottom lip as
You quiver with anticipation...

And now we both know why
Sometimes...Yeah... Sometimes

I want to be THAT guy!

"The Bad Influence"

~Z~

Lamented Love Letters

The words spoken by
A man that she had never
Met, left her heart broken
In a way that she'll never
Forget, although he has
Long been gone as she
Stumbled upon a book
Filled with every love note
That he ever wrote

Her heart bleeds again
And again as she reads
Aloud each stroke of his
Pen. Who was this man
And how can it be, that her
Heart beats, synonymously
With the one only known
Anonymously... as ~Z~

"Lamented Love Letters"

~Z~

This is a story

Filled with abundant

Intentions of

Empty Pages

For random thoughts

And tandem descensions

Into internal dimensions

That so many people

Are reluctant to share

Or even mention

Can I Wake You?

He held the door for her as they exited the concert hall with the other couple of their double date. The chilling mid-December evening had already been pleasant, but it was not over just yet. As they walked through downtown Spokane toward their cars, the woman of the other couple - with an intentionally conspicuous tone - suggested that she ride with him and that they would meet up at her apartment. They both smiled and gave each other that playful "*You bitch!*" kind of look as he opened the passenger door of his Suburban to let her in.

Once parked in front of her apartment, they open their respective doors and smile to themselves as they step out of the truck. As they approach the front of his truck, her hands reach for the hood of her jacket and he says, "Snowball fight?" She laughs and they both head for the nearest snowbank for some ammunition. He launches first but misses her. She fires back but he steps to the left just in time and the volley ensues. Unaware of his next plan of attack she turns to head toward another snowbank along the river. Before she can pack the snow in her hands into a ball, he picks her up and carries her to a larger pile of snow, one that will be much safer for her landing. His plan isn't very successful because upon throwing her into the giant pile of snow, her arms grip tightly around his neck and one of her legs wraps around one of his. They both fall into the snow and roll around laughing as they proceed to throw handfuls of snow at each other, burying one another in the frozen element that surrounds them.

"Truce" he calls as they lay there laughing, trying to catch their breath. Helping her to her feet, he pulls the collar of her jacket closed and brushes the residuals of war from her shoulders before collecting the items they'd purchased from the store. Denying his defeat, he proclaims that there is to be a rematch very soon and he can't help but notice the incredible smile upon his face as he watches her walk a few feet ahead. He's not able to see her face, but he knows that she is smiling too. Following her up the stairs to the landing in front of Apt 208, he takes the bags from her cold hands so that she can find her keys and unlock the door. She pauses for a moment, glancing at him with eyes that seem to have something to say. The look is both intentional and hesitant; yet still whispers that this could be the beginning of something special. It's in the light of her smile. Though lips can often be deceiving, no lies can be kept when her smile resides within her eyes. She invites him in for a moment before heading upstairs for dinner and drinks with the neighbor couple from earlier.

Shots of Fireball increased her feistiness, so he asked if she was ready for that rematch. She eagerly accepted so they both headed for the door and started walking down the stairs. Her ex-boyfriend, who had been outside keeping a close eye on them since they returned from the concert, was lying in wait. She stopped halfway down but he continued down the stairs to stand face-to-face with her ex, making it clear that she was protected and safe from harm. Colorful words were shared between the two men and her former partner made several threats although they were hollow and transparent. Once the ex-boyfriend left, the two decided that their rematch would have to be postponed and they went back up to the neighbor's apartment to continue enjoying the evening.

When the evening came to an end, he walked her down toward her apartment to say 'Goodnight' before continuing on his way to the parking lot where they had left his truck just before engaging in their playful war. As she unlocked the door, they heard a voice from the parking lot. "So, it's like that? You're fuckin' him now?!" It was her ex again so they both, instead, just proceeded into her apartment and locked the door to keep her safe and avoid the conflict entirely. As he encouraged her to simply ignore the bullshit, the doorknob jiggles and then BOOM! The ex-boyfriend kicked the door so hard that the frame splintered, and the hinges came loose, leaving her front door severely damaged, and then he disappeared. The neighbor couple from earlier came down to see what was going on and the police were called because the security of her home as well as the safety of her children had been compromised. When the statements had been given, the report had been made and the police had gone - that not so inconspicuous neighbor chimed in again, "By the way she says you'll be staying with her for the night!" and that playful look between the two women that previously had been exchanged upon leaving the concert venue was back. A quick, flirtatious glance in his direction preceded her response to the neighbor woman as she asserted her defense "I was going to tell him myself!"

Once the dust settles, they relax and put in a movie - sitting close to one another on her couch. It's late and they don't make it too far into the movie before she says that she's tired and is going to bed. With a pleasantly inviting tone she offers for him to join her but quickly follows that with a playfully sarcastic counteroffer saying "... unless you feel more comfortable sleeping on the couch." She continues down the hall while he just sits there for a moment, smiling at her playfulness. As he lies in her bed, he is fully aware of his intentions to show his respect for her. They are close, but both safely guarded by a few inches of seclusion. They talk lightly as she begins to fade. His nerves are hesitant, and his heart rate increases as his hand runs through the hair above her ear. He says, "Pssst, are you sleeping?" She nods softly. He continues, "Can I wake you?" and she mumbles "huh-uh" but it's playful, both indecisive and inviting. He runs soft fingers through her hair once more and caresses her cheek with his thumb as the embrace of his hand gently encourages her to lift her head from the pillow just enough for his lips to find hers. The lingering depth of his soft kiss reveals the effect she has on his soul. Sounds of soothing bliss reveal the effect he has on hers. Her hand reaches for his face as her soul replies to his message. A passion ignites but not one that burns hot with erotic intention. It's a passion that fills them both with a warm revelation to the possibilities of what lies ahead for them. They will surely succumb to a four-letter devotion who's name she forbids me to mention... their first kiss was the beginning of something special indeed.

~Z~

Sick Days

Leaving his apartment, she frantically opened her purse to find her keys because she was dangerously close to being late for work. Inside, she found the Burt's Bees Peppermint Lip balm that reminded her of his lips and consequently she subconsciously began gliding it across her own. Continuing her search, she found herself distracted by several things. The first book of the 50 Shades trilogy with a birthday inscription that he left inside the cover page and a black tie with royal blue and silver graffiti that swirled throughout the design, which he used to keep the trilogy together when it was delivered to her workplace as a surprise birthday gift. Below that was a bottle, which she had - *ahem* - stolen from his bathroom, of the mouth-watering scent that his body often left behind on her sheets and her pillows.

Next, her hand closed around a silk nightgown with black lace and elegant black feather-like designs printed against a shimmering silver background. This made her think of the matching bottoms that he had ravenously ripped open from her hip the night before, which incidentally reminded her that she would need to be extremely careful today as she would consequently be vulnerable to exposure until after work. She paused, smiling at the recollection of the evening that they had just spent together as well as this morning's playfulness, of which the lingering effects still make themselves well known within her thoughts and throughout her body. Others may be able to see the evidence written across her face, but she can *feel* it more prominently than they can see it - due to the many involuntary contractions in-between her thighs.

Digging deeper she found: a small hair clip, a few bobby pins, travel size bottles of lotion and hand sanitizer, a pack of Wrigley's Extra Polar Ice chewing gum, an older generation iPhone that her friend had given to her, a small bottle of Ed Hardy perfume (the one that drives him crazy), a receipt for the dinosaur that she recently bought for her son Xavier, and a shopping list with the listings: *chicken nuggets, french fries, chocolate milk, pickles, apple juice, hazelnut coffee, hazelnut creamer,* and a new favorite, *Almond Joy creamer,* which was the influence of her latest addiction. Buried at the very bottom of her purse, of course, she found the keychain that her daughter Amanda had made for her which bears only one key for her apartment and another for her car.

She opened the car door, got in, and started the engine to let it warm up. Taking a deep breath while trying to control the urges that swirled inside, she leaned forward to fix her hair in the rearview mirror when she was caught off-guard by his reflection as he stared back at her, wearing a plain white t-shirt and those incredibly soft pajama pants that she loved so much. Sipping coffee from the cup in his right hand and holding up the cup in his left, he was calling her back inside. She knew this man was trouble, a bad influence that she would have a very hard time trying to ignore. Nevertheless, she retrieved her Ed Hardy perfume, misting her neck and chest before turning the car off and reaching for the door handle. Smiling to herself she said, "Looks like I'll be callin' in sick today..."

~Z~

Peaceful Serenity

Sitting at a campus library cubicle with headphones plugged into my phone, I rummage through notebooks full of random thoughts, amongst many other students doing similar things. A mellow playlist brings peace to my mind as I read from excerpts given to me in my Creative Writing class. The playlist consists of mostly smooth jazz. All of its separate instruments sing with sounds much more crisp-and-clean than that of the majority of today's music. Much of the lyrics are in French, which I don't understand and that's okay because it allows me to detach from subconsciously singing along.

I'm able to read short stories, poetry, and instructional advice without distractions. The conversations, the sounds of computer keys and their fluctuating speeds, the visual freeway traffic of college students as they rush around trying to prepare for their next class; all of these things are extinct through the calming sounds streaming into my ears. This reminds me of being in love.

The last time I was in love with someone it was such a deep and fulfilling love, a captivating love. Together we had two 3yr-olds, two 8yr-olds, and a 10yr-old. You can imagine the chaos that ensued some days. A hungry, thirsty, and needy circus of elephants, monkeys, dancing bears, trapeze artists, tight rope walkers and other such entertainers all packed in our tribe of five children; running, laughing, playing, and fighting amongst the screaming volume of a Disney movie that struggled to compete with them - yet, even all of that was no match for the bond that existed between the two of us.

My eyes never leave her gaze as my hands caress and massage her shoulders before running my fingertips down the inside of her arms to her wrists. This sends tingling waves throughout her body making her shiver and squirm. I soothe her nerves with strong hands roaming up over her thighs, across her hips and up along her ribcage. She responds with her soft hands. Starting at my shoulders she begins to trace her fingertips lightly over my skin, up my neck, to my scalp where she swirls her fingers like little go-carts on a race track an then she begins tracing the features of my face and lips before making her back down, across my shoulders, along the length of my arms to my fingers where she wraps them in hers as my face rests upon the sweet, silky skin of her abdomen... and that is where I find peaceful serenity.

~Z~

A Violent Silence

So, I'm walking down the street when I begin to hear a beautiful sound coming from an orchard nearby. As I make my way through the bountiful fruit trees, I notice one that didn't have any fruit or even leaves on its branches, just a black birdcage dangling from a vacant limb. Inside was an absolutely beautiful bird, with a chain attached to her leg. Looking around for some kind of explanation, I realized there was nobody in sight. She'd been left there, locked in this cage and neglected. So, I broke the lock, opened her cage, and removed the chain that held her bound to this dark destiny. She was so happy and grateful to be free.

From then on, she flew next to me everywhere I went, singing the beautiful song that I heard the day I found her in that orchard. I wanted to show her the world she'd been missing. A world of respect, love, appreciation, happiness and excitement for what each new day brings. She proved to be just what I needed in my life as well. I woke up smiling every day and watched in amazement as she flew around singing her song.

One day she flew farther away than she had previously gone during the past few weeks. She began to fly farther and farther away each day until one day she didn't come back. Days, weeks, and months passed. I became both sad and worried for her, so I decided to take a trip through the very same orchard where I found her that day and to my surprise there she was swaying back and forth in that black iron cage. Only this time the door was open, and the chain rested not around her leg but in her beak. She was there *Voluntarily*! I was confused, dumbfounded, absolutely lost in disbelief! When I asked her "Why? Why would you

CHOOSE to come back to this place?" she did not answer, just stared at me blankly with the chain in her mouth. Her beautiful song could no longer be heard, her feathers were dingy and ragged. Her eyes no longer told of her happiness. To think, she *chose* to live in this dark destiny...

Yet here I stand, helpless, confused, and without the slightest understanding I look around, trying to find a direction in which to travel now...

~Z~

The ABC Format

After going through a collection of thoughts and memories, she began to question whether she had made the right choice. Believe it or not, she *knew* which one of them would've made her happy for the rest of her life. Cherished moments slapped her in the face for making such a foolish mistake. Drops of sadness fell from her cheeks. Everything she could have ever dreamed of, she had in a new man. Fearing this unfamiliar feeling of such a strong love caused her to make a quick and hasty decision to go back to the father of her children.

Going on that trip to Seattle for Father's Day was a huge mistake. He seemed like a completely different guy; one that seemed to care about her, as well as their children, much more than he had in the past few years. It didn't take long, though, before she found herself back in the manipulation and abusive control of the relationship that she had worked so hard to free herself from.

Justifiably disgusted with the path that her decision had set out for her, she decided to take her mind off of it for a while by making something to eat. *"Kitchen"* she exclaimed in a vigorous attempt to distract herself as she made her way through the house, though that plan backfired because the kitchen brought back so many memories of the man that came in and made love to her soul. Little blips of how much they bonded through cooking together. Making mouth-watering meals like her special mushroom and chicken enchiladas, his deliciously spicy spaghetti, or their first attempt at spinach stuffed chicken with broccoli sautéed in butter and the unattainable secret recipe for his mashed potatoes with toasted wave-caps. Nothing, though, seemed to beat the warmth she felt inside when sharing a fresh-brewed pot of hazelnut coffee with this man. Obviously, there was the one and only exception, her new addiction, an Almond Joy creamer that he had introduced to her.

Poor Ashleigh, she was dancing on the edge of a cliff, dangerously close to falling into an ocean packed with emotion. Quickly she put the coffee to her lips to avoid breaking into tears. Rescued effortlessly by the memory of his lips when the caress of coffee bathed hers in the comfort of this man's embrace. Soothing, gentle, warm, knee-weakening kisses that commanded her inner peace are just a glimpse of the amazing things he did with his lips. Teasing herself with small sips while closing her eyes to relive each moment as vividly as possible.

Under her breath, she whispered to herself some of the things he used to say to her. Vibrantly, her inner soul began jumping up and down as she smiled enormously upon hearing the echoes of how he would describe her smile to others as residing within her eyes. Wondering where he is now, she questions if she wants to try and contact him. Xavier, her son, jumped into her lap and then hugged her tightly, instantly snapping her out of a place of anxiety filled with troublesome and indecisive thought. *"Yes, yes I do and yes I will..."*

"Zebadiah?" she vehemently, yet softly, exclaims when he answers her phone call upon the third ring.

~Z~

Stargazing

Amongst the barn-colored paint chips flaking from the dry drift-wood-like deck behind our house, my 5yr old daughter lays, tucked in the apex of my shoulder like a puppy snuggled into the warmth of its mother's scruff. "*Daddy, you count those ones and I'll count these,*" she says. We begin connecting the dots with our fingertips bouncing around through the midnight backdrop behind a sea of glitter.

The infinite quantity of stars seemingly matched by the number of times we laugh at each other for losing count and having to start over. The laughter wakes me from a dream that wasn't so much a dream as it was the bedtime story that my 8yr old daughter read to me from her collection of memories:

"*Daddy, do you remember the night we laid out on the deck and counted the stars?*"
I just smiled and replied, "*Yes, baby... I do!*"

~Z~

Escape

Sitting on a drum set stool, set just inches from a 4' tower cabinet. Enclosed are two 15" speakers and a 10" vocal horn. Your hands - numb from the tightness of your grip on the upper corners of this amplified speaker cabinet. You can feel the many circular embossed areas of your forehead trying to fight their way through the metal perforated screen that reads "Peavey" as your heart tries to return to the days you were here watching this display of musical genius "live."

Your left leg - bounces rapidly, involuntarily, and upon that realization you also notice that subconsciously you wore all red and black today which were his favorite colors. Tell me that doesn't strike you as coincidental. The pain runs through your body as wild, chaotic, and free as his fingers when he manipulates the guitar strings. Every note - seeming to scream the words that you cannot. Your stomach muscles - tense and jolt as your soul bleeds.

No one is around to see the disaster you're in, but you prefer it this way because you're free to let it all out, to let it all go. You don't want comfort. You don't want relief. You want to hurt - SO BAD that your soul hardens and is no longer weak to the feeling of this pain. At the same time, you wish this inanimate 4' amplified speaker cabinet, with so much life screaming from inside, would just reach out and grab you, squeezing you back just as tightly as you're squeezing it.

Have you ever had so much inside you that the only way to get it out is the tense tightening of every muscle in your body as you squeeze the life out of someone who is in return squeezing the life out of you? It's the freedom of such suffocation that doesn't allow the gasp for air that your lungs need to proceed with the tears that fall and the pain that just won't let go.

Take me back, Peavey, to the days when I can breathe again; when I can open my eyes, and this is no longer past tense...

~Z~

This is a story

Filled with abundant

Intentions of

Empty Pages

For random thoughts

And tandem descensions

Into internal dimensions

That so many people

Are reluctant to share

Or even mention

Kids are like Botox for the Soul

Kids are like Botox for the Soul

If you don't have any, you should get some! They may run you down and make you old on the outside, but INSIDE they're what keep you young and healthy. My 8yr-old was playing on the bleachers at the football field, slipped and hit the corner of her eye on one of them. No, that's not the funny part! She ended up with a small but deep contusion on the outside corner of her eye. It was bright blue and had an indentation from the corner of the bleacher through the center.

When she woke up this morning her upper eyelid was swollen and starting to change colors. On the way out of the house I was playing with her, saying things like "Are you gonna tell them you didn't eat your dinner, so I punched you in the eye?" - "No" she said. "You gonna say you ran into a doorknob or that I pushed you down the stairs?" – again she said "No" and she laughs. Then Nathanial says, "Are you gonna tell them your little sister farted on your pillow?" ... And THAT'S when it happened!! Esperanza snaps back with the response "That's how you get PINK eye, not BLACK eye!"

And this is why kids keep you young and healthy inside! Go out right now and get you some! ... Two at least, more if you feel so inclined.

~Z~

Affirmative Affection

When the arms of a woman wrap around your neck, you get a sense of security. When the hands of a woman caress your face, you get a sense of soothing peace. With the right woman, any man can feel this...

It's when you wake up to the arm of your 3yr-old daughter pushing its way between your neck and your pillow, to embrace you as her tiny little hand caresses your face before rolling out of bed to terrorize the house, that you get a completely different feeling... the feeling that, as a father, you must be doing something right. You've shown her love and compassion - and the right ways to communicate these things. Then you smile as you roll out of bed to find dolls, toys, and books all over the house with a cartoon movie playing in the background... ahhhh yes...

She's still your 3yr-old tornado of a baby-girl!!!

~Z~

The Calm before the Storm

As I lay there, sore and exhausted, thinking about how great it would be to have a woman around who sees how hard I work and offers to give me a massage or show some sort of understanding... my 8yr-old daughter says "Dad, can I walk on your back or give you a massage?"... ahhh, the life of a single dad sometimes has a way of providing acknowledgement for how hard it can be!

And then your 3yr-old daughter throws her arms around your neck, crying hysterically and clinging to you. She is barely able to get out the words "No Daddy, I don't want you to go to work! I want you to stay here!" and you are once again reminded of the struggles that come along with being a single dad... Who needs amusement parks when you're on the endless mental and emotional roller coaster of parenthood?

~Z~

Wrapped Around Her Pinky

The vocabulary that my 3yr-old has is both amazing and dangerously powerful!

She called me last night to say "Daddy, *I need you here to lay with me...I'm sad 'cause I want you here...My eyes are watery!*"

You can only imagine how quickly I wanted to return to that time clock and swipe my badge once more...but I told her to grab the blanket her mom had given to her the last time she saw her and lay down, that I'd be there when she woke up. She agreed, not too reassuringly, but she agreed. And in the a.m. when she awoke, there I was, and all peace had been restored.

~Z~

They're Always Watching

Subconsciously harmonizing to a Sam Smith track while my oldest daughter stands next to me, leaning on my shoulder... and she says "Dad, how do you sing that good? You sound just like him!"

Those moments when you realize your kids look up to you even when you don't know they're watching... Be sure to give them a quality role model, someone they'll WANT to be when they grow up!

~Z~

When all else fails, try your hand at sales

When all else fails, try your hand at sales!!!

TREAT YOURSELF TUESDAY!!!

1- housekeeper: Deep cleaning, dishwashing, vacuuming, rearranging, and reorganizing. Let my son give you a brand-new home!!!

1- gym membership: ohhh, the calories you'll burn chasing this one around all day!!! She wrestles, kick-boxes, plays fast-paced tag, sneaks, terrorizes, and will definitely put you thru the ringer!!!!

1- relaxation treatment: she gives back massages, foot rubs (lotion optional), cuddles, clings, and even sings to you!!!

ALL YOURS AND ALL FOR THE LOW, LOW PRICE OF......... FREEEEEEEEE!!!!!!!

Tomorrow only, 3am-2pm, so hurry and call or text now!!!

~Z~

El Sol: The Sun

It is the core of our solar system, right? In a sense you could say that life itself revolves around it. It shines brighter than anything else we know and is also known for its ability to bring extreme warmth to everything that it touches.

Every day it cuts through the cold darkness of the night, shedding light onto our very existence, allowing each of us to see each other and everything that gives proof to what we call *life*. It has been said that without the sun all life on this planet would eventually fade away.

Now, I come from Mexican-Apache descent on my father's side and in Spanish we call the sun *El Sol*. It is pronounced just like the English word soul. Although spelled differently, they sound the same and if you take all of the characteristics that I just gave you for the sun (El Sol) and applied them to your soul then you might find it interesting that they are exactly the same!

So with each new rising of the sun, be sure to let your soul shine just as bright and allow it to do all of the things that it was meant to do!

Just a glimpse into the mind of

~Z~

Two Can Play at That Game

Two Can Play at That Game

Remember playin' tag as a kid? There was always someone who claimed that you never caught them. Eventually it wasn't fun for the one doing the chasing anymore. How about duck-duck-goose? It didn't matter if you were the one chasing or being chased because you knew that very shortly you would have the chance to do either one of them again. It's the back and forth that keeps it alive and keeps it fun!!!

That concept doesn't change when you get older. Sometimes you're the one being chased but keep in mind that sometimes you've got to be the one doing the chasing. A way to really step up your game is to challenge your lover by showing them *'two can play at that game'*... Ladies, if he sends you sexy little texts while you're apart, trying to tease or seduce you with the things he'd like to be doing to you while you're at work *"two can play at that game!"* If you come home to candles, flowers, and a delicious dinner for two - *"two can play at that game"* too...

Knock-knock... Who is it? - A beautiful woman with his favorite coffee in hand! Whatever it is that he does to show you how much you mean to him every day, show him you can do it too. Don't let it become a one-sided game. There's something extremely sexy about a woman who pays enough attention to the things that a man does to show how he feels about her and also cares enough to throw them back at him in a playful gesture that says, "Game on baby!"

Another little look inside the mind of

~Z~

Choose Your Words Wisely

Chelsey:
*Words to avoid in an argument when a confrontation is
Not intended... Always, Never, Can't, Won't, You.*

Me:
*Unless of course you use them wisely... "I'll ALWAYS listen
and NEVER interrupt. Silence CAN'T solve the issue, but fighting
WON'T solve it either. And when all is said and done, I'll still
love YOU!"... G'nite Miss Chelsey*

Chelsey:
*You, sir, are a scholar and a gentleman! Lol well said...that
couldn't have been said in a more appropriate time! G'nite*

One more look at what you can find inside the mind of

~Z~

Personalize Your Gifts

Take some two-tone epoxy and glue one vase inside another. Choose a flower she loves, at least two colors of ribbon, accent rocks, and food coloring for the inner vase.

Then throw in a simple fish with elegant fins that compliments the colors you've chosen... And what do you get? A custom arrangement that will make her smile all day! Happy birthday Miss Whitney!!

I've always felt that store-bought arrangements are far too impersonal and that there is much more translated in something you take the time to create.

It says things like:

- *"I know you! More than any florist"*
- *"There's a connection to each piece that I chose, and I chose them specifically for you!"*
- *"There are not 10-15 of these sitting on a retail shelf or in anyone else's possession! It's the only one! And it's for YOU!"*

~Z~

Stargazer Lily in a double vase with a
Blue Betta swimming around the internal
vase

The Gaillardia (Arizona Sun Daisy)

The Gaillardia (Arizona Sun Daisy)

I have a friend whose birthday happens to be today, and she is spending it here in Spokane instead of back in the AZ, so I thought:

"If she can't make it down to Arizona for her birthday, then I'll just bring the Arizona Sun to her!"

Not such an easy task. See, the Gaillardia is a perennial and doesn't bloom in this cold-ass weather... so I built her a custom arrangement to resemble one such blossom using green mums in the center, surrounded by red roses which were then surrounded by yellow roses and mums of a red/yellow mixture helped blend the whole thing together.

I also gave her a starter that she can plant at her new apartment, and it will bloom next season.

Happy Birthday Miss Ashley!

~Z~

Custom Floral Arrangement intentionally
designed to resemble a Gaillardia
(Arizona Sun Daisy)

Her First Real Valentine's Day

Her First Real Valentine's Day!!

(the foot work)

- a six-city search for a white dove - from Spokane to Post Falls, Coeur d'Alene, Moses Lake, the Tri-Cities, Seattle, and back over to Coeur d'Alene where I found one. Finally, an entire day's worth of phone calls, to every bird and pet shop across the state, had paid off.
- a simple Craigslist search would reveal the perfect antique-style wrought iron cage.
- a mirror, some small pine tree branches for perches, and a piece of driftwood to give the interior a little touch of home.
- a small wooden panel, some black stain, and a couple chains to build a trap door at the bottom for the tray. Stain allows you to keep the grain of the wood as opposed to covering it up with paint.
- a few hand-picked ivy plants personally set in the perfect planter and intertwined to cascade down from the top of the cage.
- finished off with white rose pedals covering the floor of the cage to signify purity and innocence, along with a few personal touches and there it is - a custom, one of a kind Valentine's Day gift. All snuck in and set up in her home while she just "happened" to be out with a friend for breakfast... It's what I do baby!

A little excessive and over the top? - Maybe, but to have never experienced a meaningful Valentine's Day at 27yrs. old? ... It HAD to be done! See, to her the Dove represents freedom. Though she's taken a few steps in the right direction, she still has quite a journey ahead of her – a lot of work in strength, self-confidence, self-identification, and independence before she can truly fly free and healthy. The cold, black, wrought iron cage is the perfect depiction of the darkness that has held her captive for 10 yrs. So, I built this gift with faith and understanding. I give it to her as the final step toward her freedom. When the time comes, and she truly feels free, she can use this as a physical representation of her freedom. Taking this step, and releasing the dove, will not only allow her to feel her freedom but it will be significant to her successful completion of a long journey to "set HERSELF free!" ***This is her Freedom Bird***

~Z~

A Dove for Her First Real Valentine's Day... her very own Freedom Bird. Customized, personalized, and surrounded by Playboy Floribundas - each tied to an image that illustrates the design process of her special gift

"There's Somethin' Happening Here... What it is Ain't Exactly Clear"

"There's Somethin' Happening Here...
What it is Ain't Exactly Clear"

As I was loading my van with some groceries, to deliver to someone in need, a woman appeared and said:

"Knock-knock, I'm guessing that you're doing something generous for someone?"
"Yes, I am"
"My name's Sheila" and she held out her hand. I took her hand in mine and said, "Zebadiah." She smiled as she repeated my name to herself and continued, "I'm celebrating the opening of my new business. I want you to have this."
"Thank you" I replied, smiling as I accepted the rose and the card.
"Thank YOU, and God bless you!" Then she walked away.

It was a rare moment for which I was unprepared and now a little unaware of how to accept what just happened. Was she simply a woman promoting her business by randomly selecting people throughout the day to hand roses to? Or a messenger sent by someone I knew? Was this "a sign" that I should look into (because we all know how often we tend to lean on Faith in moments like this) or should I just listen to the voice inside my head telling my mind to "shut it down" and just accept it as a return of the things that I often do for others?

My mind argues, "But what if..." and then attempts to find every possibility on which I would be missing out if I don't at least consider the deeper meanings to what just happened.

~Z~

Random Rose handed to me by a
woman I had never met - the new
business owner of Spectrum Dating

An Easter Story

My grandfather was Danish, and I don't know much about his religious standing. Mi Abuelita, my grandmother, was born Mexican-Apache and raised Catholic. Her favorite holiday was Easter and so her favorite flower was justifiably the Easter Lily. Every year I take some to her, a tradition I took over for my father when he lost his leg and became unable to. It fascinates me that the angle of the sun always drops a shadow of the lilies over her name! Even more fascinating is a connection that my brain put together as I planted them this year. Easter is a story of death and resurrection, which inspired faith... a sacrifice of death for an abundance of new beginnings.

The pinecones are something I also set there every year. The story goes that after he passed, and they were laid next to each other, two pinecones fell from the tree and landed on each of their names. My father kept one and his sister kept the other. If you don't know the cycle of a pinecone, or its purpose, then I'll fill in the connection for you. In 2003 I moved home to Califas. Unfortunately, the San Bernardino mountain-fires hit hard that year and, due to the Bark Beetle infestation, a large part of the mountain was wiped out! I was trippin' out on it until an older friend of mine made the comment that it was actually beneficial to the life of the mountain. See, a pinecone holds an abundance of new beginnings within itself. Under extreme heat, such as a forest fire, it explodes and spreads these new beginnings throughout the earth.

So, with much of the mountain dying from the infestation of Bark Beetles, this fire would replenish the forest with new trees... Life, death, resurrection, new beginnings... Faith!!

Just another small look inside the mind of

~Z~

Easter Lilies, Pinecones, and a shared
symbolism of New Beginnings

Embrace Your Pain and Inner Conflicts

It's been said that some of the most brilliant artists of any medium are also the most mentally and emotionally disturbed; that it's the pain or conflict inside them that makes their art form untouchable.

My father introduced me to a movie as a young teenager, "The Crossroads." A kid who's a genius classical guitar player wants to learn the blues, so he hooks up with a blues harmonica player who tells him "You'll play better blues when you've hurt more."

Often times you'll find that the deepest conflict within yourself breeds the deepest, most honest and amazing art - whether the medium be vocals, composing lyrics, poetry, musicianship, drawing, painting, photography, etc.

So, Embrace It and Create Art to Share with Others!

~Z~

This is a story

Filled with abundant

Intentions of

Empty Pages

For random thoughts

And tandem descensions

Into internal dimensions

That so many people

Are reluctant to share

Or even mention

BIOGRAPHY

As a six-year vested member of the Laborers Union (Local 238) and a fifteen-year vested member of a secret society of single father's – Zebadiah is now a thirty-eight-year-old man who set out on what he thought was a noble path at the age of thirteen, only to find out that he would eventually become the very target of his journey. Dianna was the original driving force behind that journey, as she was murdered by the hands of an abusive ex-boyfriend in May of 1997 and it was the inconceivable loss of the first woman Zebadiah had ever loved that sent him on the path of devoting the next seventeen years of his life toward advocating against domestic violence, teaching people how to see the signs of manipulation, and educating people on cultivating a healthier understanding about true respect, appreciation, love, companionship, growth, and freedom.

During that time, he spent eleven of those years in two separate relationships, each one landing him in the role of a single father. He had two children with the first woman and a third child with the next. Neither of the women from within those relationships could ever seem to fully walk away from their previous, toxic, lifestyles of drug and alcohol abuse, so Zebadiah respected their freedom of choice but refused to let them drag him and their children along for the ride. Though the years that he spent raising children alone, both during and after those relationships, proved to be a challenge – the hardest thing for him to cope with was the realization that he had become the very target of his original path. Three years of creative writing taught him how he ended up there, why he made the choices he made, and what he had to do in order to change that behavior. He also learned how to have a deeper understanding of who he is, who he wants to be, what he wants for the future of his family, and what kind of partner he wants by his side – growing with him.

Throughout the next six years, following his three-year journey, he used - and continues to use - what he has learned about himself to pursue much healthier relationships with all of the people that he chooses to have in his life. He found a strong hunger for personal growth across all planes. He now focuses on utilizing any mental and emotional turbulence - in various, positive ways - as fuel to drive his deep desire to maintain a healthy path of forward progress in all areas of his life. The long-awaited production and self-publication of this book, through his newly established business and multifaceted LLC, are just a few examples of how he has harnessed that energy.

Zebadiah Sprague
Illustrious Illustrations LLC

"Education. Understanding. Growth. Positivity. Creative Arts and Expression. Find these things within yourself and then shed the Light of who you are onto the rest of the world."

~Z~